*2014 Annual*

I0475887

# Freelance
# Success Stories

## How to Get Online Jobs, Earn Big Profits, and Work from Home

**Nick Passig**

Rio World Class

Denver, Colorado USA

Published by Rio World Class, Denver, Colorado.
Published simultaneously in Canada.
www.RioWorldClass.com

ISBN 978-1-312-13048-7

Printed in the United States of America
Annual Edition


Editorial Vision and Design by Nick Passig
www.NickPassig.com

# Table of Contents

Dedicated to those who compete
with what they are capable of —

# Introduction

Dear Reader,

Are you getting the success you want out of your current freelance career?

If the answer is no, I can help you get greater satisfaction and pay from doing the work you like to do. I've done it for other freelancers around the world, I think I could do it for you too. At the very least, I'm offering a way to find out without risking more than the price of this book.

I know you've been thinking about becoming independent, or changing careers so you can move up to a more advantageous position in your life.

I share the awareness of what a small improvement in your career can mean to you. That's why I'm writing this book.

I've made arrangements for you to read the following freelancer success stories. Why am I doing this? One simple reason.

In my opinion, you can't possibly know the recipe for online freelance success unless you read these heartwarming and insightful stories.

The virtual workforce is growing. Millions of people are competing for the limited freelance jobs that are available.

If you're like most freelancers, you desire to work in the 'virtual office' with your 'virtual team'.

I'm here to tell you that many freelancers are achieving their dreams by working directly from home using an Internet-connected computer.

This book is unique because it offers unique perspectives from virtual workers who have actually succeeded. They have succeeded regardless of their background, circumstances and regardless of where they live.

If you desire online jobs in the global workforce —and working from home is what you want to do, then this might be the book for you.

The primary goal of this book is to give you the recipes of success through personal stories. These Internet-based contractors are men and women, just like you and me, who wanted to get more jobs, earn more money, and improve their living conditions.

The contractors featured in this book wanted to improve their own lives and ride the emerging 'virtual office' trend. They realized that there is a <u>skill</u> to develop that will help them to prosper in the future —here's the space-age <u>skill</u> I am talking about:

*Working from home over the Internet.*

The freelancers in this book are proof that with an Internet connection, one can work from just about any country in the world.

These freelancers have also enjoyed the other huge benefit of being able to work at their own convenience on things that they enjoy doing.

In the developed world, new college graduates dream of the "suitcase job" —where they can travel to exotic vacation destinations while working from a laptop computer. In the under-developed world, a whole new economy is springing up and fundamental training programs are just getting underway.

From the success stories offered in this book, you can learn success strategies while avoiding the pitfalls of failure. These stories offer inspiration and ideas that you can use in your journey to the top.

The people who share their stories are entertaining, inspiring, and offer timeless lessons to freelance workers in any situation.

The evolution of the global workforce market is moving fast like a freight train. Those who try to ride this train either fail or succeed. For many virtual contractors, their first virtual contracting job is the first train ticket to their next career destination. Whether you are a seasoned contract professional or an expert-in-training, this book will have something for you.

As a business consultant and media entrepreneur, I am grateful for the opportunity to write this book, compile the contributor's stories and ultimately share this information with the world. I am planning to release this book annually if the readers find it useful.

The preparation for this book took several years. I would like to explain why it took me so long to produce this book and why I may be particularly suited to put it together.

Many years ago, I was a talent recruiter for large multinational corporations. My job was to find new workers for open positions in my clients' businesses. During this time, I had face-to-face interviews with over 2,000 job applicants. It was in this time, that I became well skilled at finding and interviewing new freelance professionals.

Within a short time, this skill carried over very well to the Internet consulting world. In various high-level positions, I was able to interview and hire multiple offshore firms. This was important for me to learn how to use large outsourced teams for serious projects.

In addition to that, I interviewed, hired, and trained hundreds of freelancers for my own projects. During this time of interviewing, hiring, and training thousands of people, you might say I have learned a few helpful lessons. Most of the lessons are summed up in the stories of these international freelancers.

It's no secret that the largest companies in the world have already outsourced much of their work to contractors and temporary employees. And with the growing supply of online freelance marketplaces, the specialization of Internet-workers continues, and the expansion of the virtual worker market continues.

Some experts speculate that half of the jobs at Fortune 500 companies will be outsourced by 2020. The ramifications of the virtual contractor trend are global. This is why I encourage anyone who plans to be working with computers to pay more attention to this trend —and better yet —embrace it completely.

It's no surprise that the outsourcing opportunity drives jobs from more developed countries to less developed countries. This has positive and negative effects on the involved economies. Jobs are flowing from one country to another, money is flowing from one to another, competition is skyrocketing, unemployment is wavering, all while human workers are being replaced by automation.

In this author's opinion, developed countries may want to re-consider the mandatory minimum wage for home country workers, because removing this barrier would open up new job opportunities that could not have existed due to wage minimums. Also, businesses may need to be prepared for stifling regulations on outsourcing in an effort to better regulate the employment markets.

On the positive side, we have never experienced a world so connected. We are seeing upstart entrepreneurs on every continent who are tapping into the freelance talent in order to pursue lifelong dreams. The changing environment and competitive evolution is happening whether we like it or not.

About The Featured Freelancers

Recently we gathered together a group of international virtual contractors and asked them for their tips, strategies, and struggles while working as Internet-based workers. In this book, we kindly offer these stories to you as inspiration and revelation.

Within each story are important lessons; much is to be learned through the inspiration, struggles, and success stories of these contributors. They have shared their personal and professional challenges in the hope that they may help someone who dreams of career opportunities that have never been available to them before.

In addition to these success stories, many contributors offer information about industry trends, proven models for success, and the demands of current employers who are hiring them for their work. So to put it plainly, anyone who seeks excellence in their own freelance career may find valuable insights from this book.

# Meaningful Choices

People respond in equal measure to the challenges of the environment.

The following inspiring stories of international freelancers in this book will move you to find your own meaning and career direction. Just like them, you may wish to change certain circumstances in your life because you desire more.

The author has curated a large number of stories and interviewed many freelancers in order to come up with a concise set of stories that entertain and enlighten.

If you choose, you will be able to take on a new direction towards working from anywhere, working on your own schedule, and fully unlocking your potential. The results may be that you will get more freelance jobs and earn more money doing the things you love to do.

It is true that our choices match our motivations. Regardless of our profession, interests and status in life, we proceed as we are moved. Some choices are for survival and necessity, others for approval and status.

We are driven towards online freelancing for some personally significant cause...perhaps to fill up some emptiness of time...or perhaps just a chance to prove oneself. It could be an economic cause or simply self-gratification.

Individual differences extend to choices people make regardless of their station in life, geographical region, and experience.

The international freelancers featured in this book all come from different walks of life —all who approached freelancing for diverse yet very significant reasons. You will notice however, these freelancers are all good at writing. Most of them earned their first dollar researching content and writing articles.

The intent of this chapter is to show you freelancing is not that difficult nor scary and in fact may be the key that unlocks the door to your own personal success.

Without waiting another moment, let us get to know these freelancers who have shared their experience with us.

Here are some quick previews to the virtual contractors who are featured in this book:

*Sandra* wrote something to the President and received a reply. She then realized that literature is very powerful that it could be used as a tool for change.

*Jasim* is an expert in Web Development and he wants to improve his skills by applying for more jobs through freelance marketplaces. He mentioned that it's not easy to get a job online because you need to create a profile that will really impress employers.

*Umair* is a freelance writer who graduated from one of the prestigious schools in Pakistan. He actually thought that applying for a job online is not a legit way to earn income. But when he started doing it, he fell in love with it.

*Sheila* is a mom of two and is very thankful that she was introduced to oDesk.com. She was very much surprised with how much she can earn by just working at home at her own pace and at her own convenience.

*Saifur* finds his income from teaching and journalism insufficient for his needs. So he joined the other online freelancers and looked for freelance work. He believes in the line of the song —'we shall overcome someday...' And so he did!

*Noori-Shaikh*, a medical student, tried online freelancing to help her through medical school. She never thought she would be able to get a client. Her attempt gave her an experience that made her believe in herself. Thanks to her sister who introduced her to the 'virtual office'.

*Monjour* is an expert in web-based applications. This is one way he was able to find a way to use his talents online. He thought —instead of always logging into Facebook.com, he might as well go to freelance marketplaces and be productive!

*Mirijed* is a young ambitious guy who takes challenges positively and is very good at developing strategies. He appreciates virtual contractor marketplaces because he could also be exposed to different types of work.

*Kim* has authored nine books and was not into freelancing. With a few twists and turns, she ended up as a freelancer. She thinks freelancing requires commitment and of course, know how. She was able to find a way to love what she's doing while earning at the same time.

*Joanna* suffered from a medical condition. She lost her sense of hearing to meningitis but she maximized the situation by turning to reading and writing. She turned that condition into something amazing by developing other skills. Now she earns while doing the things she enjoys most. It's really awesome!

*Charles* is a freelance writer, researcher, and virtual assistant for over 11 years. He thinks that there is a great world of difference between a job application and a freelance profile. A freelance profile needs a well-stocked and up-to-date portfolio of assessments and work samples.

Different Approaches to Online Freelance

These amazing individuals approached life's challenges and were able to easily face up to extreme obstacles that a weak spirit would readily shy away from. Perseverance and strength are philosophies that made these individuals excel in what they do.

*Building a Professional Profile*

Each of these freelancers started out with building up their freelance marketplace profiles. To be noticed in the virtual worker marketplaces, a well-groomed profile is a very easy yet most significant step.

*What's in a name?*

The first thing you do is decide what name and title you are going to give yourself —basically, focused on what job position are you pursuing.

One freelancer chose this title for himself:

*Fiction writer/Creative writer/Article writer/Music artist.*

The job title is the brief showcase you can post that will give clients an idea what kind of contractor you are. The more specific your description the better for the client to know whether to hire you or not. There is, however, a downside for the freelancer to this. Writing *Fiction writer/Creative writer/Article writer* will limit you to only these three writing areas. If you are a creative writer you can obviously do a story. But it is not in your title, so the client may turn to another contractor right away. In freelancer marketplaces, you create your own title. As you will be the creator, create something attractive and comprehensive. Something that will help to match you with the opportunities you seek.

As an example, the marketplace oDesk.com has nine categories from which you can choose to create your title. These are web development, software development, networking and information system, writing & translation, administrative support, design and multimedia, customer service, sales & marketing, and business services.

For each of these categories are subcategories that will help you identify what matches your skill set. For example, customer service has four specific subcategories that includes customer service and support, technical support, phone support, and order processing.

By labeling your skills properly, you provide the best possible setup for landing higher paid jobs that you like to do.

*Different Folks, Different Strokes. . .*

You can reach the same destination from different paths. Some paths will give you the challenge but will take a lot of time, while other points may be well-paved but with lots of wayside temptations.

We can learn some things from our featured freelancers.

*Portfolio Development*

*Charles* discovered that if he approached all freelancing as a job application, his efforts will likely fail. He realized that he should have a well-stocked and up-to-date portfolio of assessments and work samples. Online employers will only know the potential of their freelance workers by reviewing the evidence of the contractor's accomplished tasks.

*Profile and Tag Lines*

*Joanna* followed her gut. While building her profile, she enumerated and described how she is very much able to deliver quality service to potential clients. She edits regularly her profile and tag lines —to be constantly fishing for new opportunities. Some marketplaces allow for pre-testing of skills. The skill test results from the tests she took proved an attraction in her profile.

*Brag a little bit*

Bragging is not as difficult for *Kim*. She already has nine books to her credit which she can showcase as evidence of her abilities. Some of you may feel a little shy to brag about your achievements. This is, however the only way you can show employers what you are.

*Saifur* presented himself as a journalist-researcher. He advises that a profile should be 100% complete and should contain important information that will catch the attention of employers. He also recommends to upload a smart picture of yourself in your profile.

*Be real*

*Monjour* feels that the profile you create must be a true reflection of your real self. So, he took tests in areas of his expertise. This made him confident that when he presents himself, he knows he is telling the truth about his expertise and himself. This works well for new contractors who have not yet earned a feedback score.

*Persistence*

It was different with *Noori*. She prepared a very simple profile that did not quite help. Her persistence in pursuing jobs and interviewing however, earned her a job that now she enjoys.

*Assessments*

*Umair* was a skeptic when it came to online freelancing. He didn't fully comprehend how people earn money from working on the internet. He wondered how one can get a job when the information you fill out online is just your name. Then he saw the most believable testimony about his own skills by taking some of the marketable skills tests. He took those he was skilled at, and wow! The test results validated his claims of expertise.

All these remarkable freelancers may be described with one word —
passion. That passion shifted their weakness into a strength that
pushed away the fear of rejection and the unknown.

It was passion that moved *Ali* to pour his thoughts into paper —an
innocent action that took him out of his difficult situation. It was
passion to do something for others that mom *Sheila* engaged herself to
write for a client. It was passion to accomplish God's "to do list" that
moved *Umair* to write, even if he is a professional engineer.

With passion and self-reliance, these contractors were able to carve out
substantial freelance businesses all their own. Here are their stories.

# Envelopes and Paragraphs

*Sandra wrote something to the President and received a reply. She then realized that literature is very powerful that it could be used as a tool for change.*

*Story by Sandra Colton*

I realized at an early age that I had been bestowed a God given gift of expression through words. At a very young age I wrote the President of the United States a letter regarding his lack of effort concerning our oceans and their quickly deteriorating marine life. I was beyond words when my mother picked me up from the bus stop one afternoon and informed me that I had received a letter from the President himself. From that moment on I realized the power of literature and the importance behind it.

True, raw and real literary expression has the power to calm the masses, ignite nations and truly inspire. That is why it is of the upmost importance that as authors we bring forth the truest reflection of our thoughts and imagination. The artistic ability to create an alternate reality or bring life to civilizations that have long since passed is more than a mere form of journalism and should be applauded; fighting our way through self-discovery, aka self-destruction, while holding onto a tiny piece of childlike enthusiasm, carrying it into adulthood, is nothing short of a miracle. Battles have ensued throughout history over the right to dream, pray, imagine and believe. Their scars of defeat linger for centuries within the individual and society as a whole. The shear preservation of the idea of possibility through the constant fight for freedom of expression should serve as reason alone to not only seek out our unbridled creative nature but embrace it, becoming truly enveloped within the curiosity of the human psyche.

Through the chase of corporate and financial ambitions it is easy to lose sight of what reality truly is. It is without question an avalanche of catastrophic and untimely events that send tidal waves through our fundamental ideals and values. No individual looks at themselves as a child and dreams of being the victim of violence or devastating circumstances. There are children carrying the burdens of this world held tightly within the grasp of their tiny hands and entire nations falling in poverty and defeat. These circumstances were created not by the world but by the shattered remnants of ourselves. The question of solution often arises when it becomes the topic of political gain, often in a matter of theatrics displayed behind a podium and a golden smile. The solution though comes not from the humble words of politicians but from the knowledge of those who live it. Their message is not heard through the echoing of a microphone it is heard, it is learned, through the words found within the tattered pages of a book.

As authors it is our divine responsibility to not simply entertain the masses but to move them. The ability to spark intrigue within the eyes of a child who has lived within the darkness of reality is in itself a glimpse into faith and divinity. You ask why I write? The answer is not within my words, it is within the voices of the world in which I seek to explore, ignite, change and belong.

*Sandra Colton*
*Professional Freelance Author*
*2006-present*
*United States*

*For more information about this contributor, view the Resources section at the end of this book.*

# First Impressions

*Jasim is an expert in Web Development and he wants to practice his profession by applying for a job online. He mentioned that it's not easy to get a job online because you need to create a profile that really impresses employers.*

*Story by Jasim Uddin*

Biography:

I'm Md Jasim Uddin from Dhaka, Bangladesh and this is the story of my freelancing career as an expert web based application developer. As a web developer, I have started freelancing to be my own boss and to share my knowledge that I have achieved through my education and professional experience.

Creating a profile:

The most important part is creating my profile. I needed to have a profile that would reflect the true 'me'. You need to have straight and realistic information when creating a profile on a freelancing platform. You need to be precise with the information and it takes a lot of care.

At the time of creating my profile, it was very important for me to choose the words to describe myself including my skill set. I wasn't able to do it at first because it's not very easy. I asked a local friend who already has created a profile and asked on what are the things that need to be written.

When I opened my account, I was thinking about what are the qualities or skills that the employers are looking for in their workers. I want to make sure that I will be chosen.

A very important aspect about the profile is not to leave it on total 'self certification'. I declare to be proficient on some tools and that is purely a self certification. So what is the way to justify my claimed expertise? There is a way —thanks to the certification test that is provided by the outsourcing platforms. By passing the tests, I can establish my claim of being an expert on the tools I have mentioned in my profile.

But taking the tests need careful planning again. What test do I need to pass as a software engineer and web based application developer? The following three aspects came into consideration on this matter which I wanted to ensure by the tests I have taken.

Profile and tests are also linked with portfolios - the samples of my work in other words. There should be harmonization among all these three and they should complement each other. I have chosen the works that best describe my skills. The portfolio is a very effective means to present myself, as nothing is better than illustration to convey the message.

Winning work:

I am newer and it's very difficult to get a single job. I got a technical writing post and that was a fixed employment. The price given was $15 if there's no error from any angle. Then I thought if I bid $1 to get in the door with the employer, then maybe I can get that job of course. Guess what? I got accepted. Once hired, I will get a message and a notification on the work marketplace.

I got my first interview in one month. I almost didn't get the job because my bid was too high. But now I have several projects for Web Development from an American employer. My hourly rate is $8 and it's not bad at all for what I could earn comparatively. Even if I have a current project; I'm also applying for another one of the same type at the same time so I could get more jobs.

Delivering the work:

Winning the work is just the start. Once I get an order, I need to do proper planning for the whole project. I like to work in a structured way where it makes me prepared to deliver as fast I can.

It is very important to keep regular communication with the employer to give updates on your work, preferably on a daily basis. There's an application you can use for hourly rate contractors designed by oDesk. This is for them to track the time you've worked, so in this case, you will be paid according to your rate. The other one is for fixed rate contractors, whom communicate about payment via message. The only thing that you need to do is upload your work and send it. For Web Development, we can upload it temporarily on a sub-domain. If the employer will give the main domain, then we can also upload on that.

Getting paid:

I believe all payments should be done through the outsourcing platform. For example, I like to get paid only through oDesk because I find it to be more secure.

Advertising Information:

I contribute a significant amount of time on freelancing platforms especially on oDesk where I apply to more and more projects (within my job application quota, of course) because it helps build my profile even if I am not awarded for the project. I don't have offline work anymore and I want use my skills here at oDesk which I've been taking seriously.

I have learned quickly, but I cannot say it was easy. In the upcoming months, I will continue to work hard and pursue more work.

*I am Jasim from Bangladesh*

*For more information about this contributor, view the Resources section at the end of this book.*

# Up the Ante

*Umair is a freelance writer who graduated from one of the prestigious schools in Pakistan. He actually thought that applying for a job online is not legit. But when he started doing it, he fell in love with it.*

Biography:

Hello, my name is Umair, another fellow looking to conquer the world, follower of imaginations and with a to-do list which God gave me. I'm from Pakistan, grew up here, and spent 17 years of my life in this country. I belong to a Muslim family. My father is Riaz Ahmed, an engineer and is currently running his own business. I'm from the city called the heart of Pakistan —Lahore. It's rich in culture, proficient in symphony and developed in all senses. I got my education in one of the most prestigious institutions of this country and am from an engineering family.  This is why I ended up doing a full-fledged course in Engineering.

With my passionate soul I look forward to every turn of my life as an experience, as a job and as a game to win. As far as my freelancer career is concerned I had a great hold on my pen, so the good God emphasized me to pick it up and do something good for others - in short I'm a freelance writer. My skills are comprised of fiction writing, script writing, story writing and a lot of article writing. When I begin to write it is like someone is whispering in my ear to carve the words on paper. This was all about my personality, till now.

Creating a profile:

When I heard of earning online for the first time I thought who in this planet would spend his/her time on the internet in search for money and who will think of it as a legit and luxurious job.  But I was wrong. Taking off all the nerve, I decided to jump into it to see if I can make of something. I created my profile online with glitter in my eyes. At first I thought of how to make a profile which merely stated my name... But again I was wrong. Gradually things started to gather up and it was finally making some sense. Then I realized the beauty of freelancing.

I then started to troll at various jobs and see how they demanded perfection. It scared me a bit but then I got the courage to hit the 'Apply' button. What I got was complete failure at first. Well who believes an amateur profile at first glance? To make it even harder there were dozens of tests on the marketplace which were a source of testimonies for the workers to the hiring clients. I decided to do the same. First of all I went with some beginners linguistics tests, some verbal and written English tests, then advanced towards some tests which focused on my basic theme "Article Writing". I tried to convince the clients with some heavy English and like I was the son of Nicholas Spark. I aimed on getting their trust and assured them of my skills. I did some sample work and reviewed some of my paperwork so that I can show it on my profile with nice scores. Then interviews showed up.

Believe me at first it was like a job in hell. Who on this planet would work all day for just $5? My point is that the first jobs weren't as handsome as I expected. But one has to go on with everything! I bore the first jobs just to gain experience which proved to be even more valuable.

<u>Winning work:</u>

Personally I was in love with the application form of freelancing websites. There were no annoying forms to be filled up and no CVs or anything like that. You simply check for all the requirements of the clients and bid for it. Well, bidding is one of the key points which makes you win a job. Tell me! Who would like to pay you $100 just to collect some pictures of a country?

The most important part is bidding generously and bidding in parallel to the job's criterion. Neither bid too small to be not neglected nor make it too much that the client goes bankrupt. Light the candle with humble hands. For some of the jobs there are well over 20 applicants and many jobs have tons of contractors each with a wish to win it. But here starts the art of a freelancer.

You've got to make yourself the most distinguished and trustful person. I personally recommend that you should provide the client with a surety of money back guarantee. Ask them to pay according to their wish. Win their trust by the facility of doing it again in case they don't like it (we call it a rewrite). Now as the client gets a ping from you and likes all the terms, it is likely for you to get a reply soon. It seems like 97% of the clients offer you an interview if you have everything well organized. If you're good with your sales pitch then it's all set.

Try to negotiate with the client about the various perspectives of the job. Make him aware of your policies and in return learn about his/her requirements. I recommend you not to be a nerd and nor act like you're straight from World Bank.

Delivering the work:

Now once you've made the deal and the job is all yours, the very next thing that comes about is how to manage? How to take your time? How to deliver? And the most important thing is how to maintain quality? For the very first time even the simplest jobs will look like hell. But the most graceful skill of a contractor is to USE THE TIME! Please don't waste your time asking questions again and again. Most clients like to only click a button and let the work be done. The contractor should abstain from any type of inconvenience for his/her dear client. Your main focus should be on getting a positive feedback. I would rather say "Money is Mortal, Feedback is immortal".

The next consideration is how to achieve the quality. Either you're doing writing work, data collection, data entry or a HTML project etc. Don't overwhelm yourself with the job. Revise your skills and pay regard to the job. Once you'll start to love the job it'll be a piece of cake for you. Create various steps and objectives for you. For instance, if you have to deliver an After Effects project of 20 videos, divide them into collections of 5. Work in batches. In this way you'll focus more on the task rather than on the load of work and will be having the potential of getting work done within a stipulated time span.

<u>Getting paid:</u>

Payment is the most important and happy part. Once the job is done you can rest your head and wait for the money to come to you. A lot of people are worried about this process. Will I get paid? How will I get my payment? Is it legit? How much does it cost? Well, freelancing payment has greatly fascinated me even if I was not a fan of online transactions (Once I suffered from a payment drop of $400). But wait! I have earned about $6000 so far and do you think I hired a genie for that? No! It was all of the effective system the freelancing sites have employed. Please note that these websites are spending their day and night and have left no stone unturned in making their payment systems effective. It is up to you on how you use it. These sites offer two types of payment modes i.e. hourly and fixed payments. I'm going to give you a brief introduction about my experience with this. Well start with hourly payments. These types of payments are much guaranteed. The employer uses virtual workstation software for monitoring all your activities and tasks and records the hours for which you've worked and pays you according to your hourly rate (the registered software is available on each freelancing site).

The clients with hourly jobs check out all the screen shots, monitor all your performances and approve of your work. The websites system then carries on the required transaction. But the complicated part comes with fixed price jobs. It's important to mention that all the freelancing sites DO NOT GUARANTEE you for fixed price jobs.

Now don't get disappointed from this policy. Fixed price jobs are actually fun to do. Freelancing sites provide you with the facility of an upfront payment. For instance, if there is a job for $100 then you can demand an upfront/advance payment of 10% and you'll get $10 in advance and you can work without any tension of not being paid for your honest work. But I recommend the milestone payment method. In this mode you create various milestones of objectives for payment. As explained earlier you can break down your project into pieces and then demand a specific price for each objective you've covered. Like if I'm on a job to translate a book of 200 pages for $40 then what I'm going to do is divide it into 50 pages and then ask for a price of $10 for each 50 pages.

By the use of correct compensation technique and improvised method, my freelancing has been favorable on me. Many people ask how much you can make out of freelancing. Well it depends upon how much do you work? There are even jobs from $10 to $10000. Some are going to take an hour and some can go on for 6 months. It all relies on how much heed you pay to your e-lancing. If you're sincere with your work then you can load your bank with money! Don't want to face the cold world? Then face the competitive online world and earn your fortune!

Advertising information:

Now marketing your skills and advertising your work plays a very important role in your freelancing career. Once you're into the marketplaces then the next subject is about preaching your quality and earning a well-known status. I would simply say that this part doesn't require that much struggle. Your main focus should be on how to provide others with beyond-satisfaction quality-work. If a client likes your work then he/she won't go anywhere in search of any other contractor when he/she has his asset (you!). As a saying "A pretty asset is considered endangered species". In other words, your work performance will advertise you itself.

Getting employers to know who you actually are and what you're capable of is what you should focus on.

I would like to provide the following summary so as to save others some of the time-consuming mistakes that I made along the way.

Focus on these key areas:

- Great feedback from previous jobs

- Complete, detailed profile

- Portfolios

- Great personality

- Cover letter writing

- Good scores at tests

- Nice approach to objective that you can communicate

- Full professional history

*Umair Ahmed*
*Freelancing career: about 2 years*
*Lahore, Pakistan*

*For more information about this contributor, view the Resources section at the end of this book.*

# Life's Everyday Mishaps

*Sheila is a mom of two and is very thankful that she was introduced to online work. She was very much surprised with how much she can earn by just working at home at her own pace and at her own time.*

*Story by Sheila Noreen Gamo*

I am actually a newbie in terms of working online. The virtual contractor marketplaces were introduced to me by a friend who claimed to earn a lot just by going online. I couldn't believe her unless I proved it to myself. You see I've been scammed by easy-earning promises before. I even tried paid-to-click sites and even set up my own web store, but at this moment none of those have really worked out for me. And recently, just this last three months or so, I have been on oDesk.com and I was surprised of how much I can earn by working at home at my own pace and time. To date (as of August 10, 2012) I have withdrawn around $300 and I still have some pending money on the site. I joined last May 30, 2012 only.

All my life I have never had a full time job. I am a Bachelor of Music graduate and majored in Music Education and Voice. Even before I graduated, I have been performing as a freelance professional stage actress and singer for the biggest companies here in our country, including our Cultural Center of the Philippines. I also was fortunate enough to have been given the chance to host children's shows and do bit roles for soap operas on TV. It was a life I enjoyed and paid well if you are able to give your full time and effort to it. But of course, it was a life of uncertainty because there were times I was sleepless and overworked and most of the times I was jobless for months. You do the math.

Soon enough, I was able to put together my own theater group SUPERVOICE MUSIC & THEATER FOUNDATION, INC. which has been running since 1995. I have trained very good actors and have put together many original musicals that earned well, whenever there was an audience. But of course this is seasonal and the competition is usually cut-throat to put it plainly. There is no money in the Theater Arts (or we do not have the marketing skills to make it work). The group is still existing, but most of the time, we are sitting ducks.

At this point, being a mother of two and living with and supporting my parents who are in their senior years, I didn't want to just sit back and relax while my husband works hard to pay all the bills for all of us. I wanted to help, but of course I didn't want to leave my kids to a nanny (it's not like I can afford one). I tried looking for work but my experiences did not match any job that would actually help pay the bills. And it meant I had to spend less time with the kids.

Well, at this point I can say working online as a creative writer has helped me pay for my own cell phone bill and I was able to chip in to pay for the electric bill as well. I was lucky to have had my first project to be a re-write of a screenplay into a stage play. It paid $200 and I was able to finish it in just a week. My client also gave me a good rating and review. This paved the way to other regular clients where I write one article a week for $10 each.

I was also lucky to have had a chance to work for another web business where I was even trusted to become the website's community manager. I enjoyed this job so I didn't mind if it paid only $1 per hour. Unfortunately, I crashed and burned when I was promoted into the general manager position. The owner of the site trusted me so much that he made me in-charge of the technical side of the site as well. I didn't say no because I wanted to test my capabilities as well. Apparently, it was too much for me and it came at a time my daughter was in the hospital. I realized I sucked when it came to computer terms and programming. I'm a music-major for Christ's sake! I begged them to take me off from the role as general manager and I continued to support the site in my own little way of promoting it to my friends. They promised to hire me again when they need my services, but that is least likely.

From then on, I got other jobs where I also learned a lot from. I accepted technical article writing projects which I hated. But I got to know how to use keywords, to research and how to use Copyscape as well. It's not like I need Copyscape. My writing is always from my mind. I guess you see that by now.

My recent job is recording scenes from screenplays. This is a study tape for an actor who is memorizing his scenes while driving his car. I enjoy this a lot and it pays $5 per hour.

My lowest pay is $0.50 per hour (10hrs/week) where I write a self-help e-book for the victims of the war in Libya. I don't mind the fee since the project is meaningful and useful to the needy.

At the beginning, I was also fooled by jobs that were bogus or shall we say scammy in nature. There is this one client who refused to hire me through the marketplace. They said they would pay me through PayPal instead. They asked for so many samples and I complied. As soon as they got the samples, I never heard from them again. Well, that's when I decided never again to accept jobs outside the marketplaces. Also, I learned never to do free work, even if they call it "samples". I've read the rules and regulations on  the marketplaces and even samples had to be paid for, even if for only a minimal fee.

I also learned to choose my clients properly. I read the ratings and comments from past contractors now and also how many they have hired in the past. I stay away from new hiring managers as much as possible.

Lastly, I choose the jobs I apply for very carefully. I make sure that I have the right talents and skills for the job. Bidding should also be reasonable to be considered for a hire. Sadly, many clients choose the lowest bidder most of the time. But in my mind, it's a "you get what you pay for".

I am thankful to have learned about online-work and will be doing this regularly from now on. I recommend it too for bright and talented stay-home moms like me.

To me, the sky is the limit. I know that online jobs are a great way to earn more income.

*Sheila Noreen Gamo*
*I have been accepting article writing jobs for the last five years.*
*Bacoor Cavite City, Philippines*

*For more information about this contributor, view the Resources section at the end of this book.*

# 21<sup>st</sup> Century Digital

*Using the internet made everything easier. There's no need for you to travel to go to work. You can just do it at home and get a good amount of money.*

*Story by Saifur Rahman Saif*

Now-a-days, outsourcing and freelancing have become two common names. Knowledge-able and educated people around the world are heading towards the freelancing jobs. Job providers too, who want their works completed within the time limits, are also approaching freelancers. There are a lot of agencies across the world that plays key roles in communcating with both job seekers and job providers. They take a lump-sum amount of money  from the job providers for bringing the job seekers closer to them using the Internet.

The modern age is called the "age of computer" as well as the "age of Internet". You cannot think of anything without the Internet. The Internet makes everything easier all across the globe. It turns the whole earth into a global village. Now, we are the citizens of the global village. Any citizens of the village can contact any person around the world within a very short span of time. But it was quite impossible a few years back. It is the internet that made the hardest thing easy.

Using the internet, unemployed and half-employed people of the world are being fully employed. They are getting handsome amounts of money, too. Time does not matter in the world of freelancing. A freelancer does not need to maintain official timetables for their jobs. They do not need to use any type of vehicle for reaching the place where he or she sells his or her labors. He or she just needs a computer with an Internet connection. But the employee needs strong commands in English as because English is the business language that helps people communicate. Educational backgrounds and skills in the related fields of jobs are needed, too. Those who want to work on software development, web designing and so on, need to have practical experiences in the related fields. Typing speeds are needed for those who want to work on data entry. And, excellent English backgrounds are needed for those who want to work in creative writing or jobs of translation. For outsourcing jobs, the incumbents need to have practical experiences rather than the certificates. Certificates play smaller roles than that of practical experiences for freelancers.

As a freelancer, I'm very sincere towards my job. I've no experience in software development or web designing. That is why; I did not try to find jobs in those fields. If I did so, I would not be able to find any job. As a creative writer I'm getting handsome jobs. I think the job providers are choosing me as they find me experienced in this field they need. I, too, think, my field of job is only creative writing and related fields. I'm a journalist in profession. I'm a school teacher, too. My vision, mission and passion are writing. That is why I wanted to have jobs in those related fields. I needed jobs other than those of teaching and journalism to make my income healthy. To make me fit in the competitive world, I needed some extra money for livelihood. I'm very much free, fair and sincere to say that prices of daily commodities in Bangladesh, my motherland, are out of reach for the general population. The trends of hiking prices of necessities were fueled by the government as it repeatedly hiked the prices of fuel, power and so on. Prices of food, clothing, construction equipment, teaching and reading materials, cosmetic goods, baby foods, utensils and every short thing are going up now and then. That is why I needed a job to meet my daily requirements.

As a journalist, I heard a lot about outsourcing. The government, too, was trying to make the educated people be involved in such jobs to curb figure of unemployment. I took the chance in that way.

I came in touch with Swanirvar Bangladesh and knew a lot about freelancing while I was trying to find such jobs. One morning, I was informed that a two-day training on Learning and Earning through Outsourcing organized by Swanirvar Bangladesh in association with the Bangladesh Government was going to be launched on that day. I was in my school at that time. So, I had to go to the principal for a leave for the time being. I joined the workshop for the first day on May 9, 2012. I took part of the workshop on the second day after school on 10th May.

It enriched my knowledge about freelancing jobs. I also got a clear idea about the registration system for freelancing jobs. The main instructor of the workshop, Khalid Noman Husainy, is a young man. He, as I observed, was sincere in his job and also during trainings. His assistant, Farzana was devoted towards her job, too.

It is the Bangladesh government that arranged the workshop for those who were searching jobs on freelancing. Around fifty youths were given the chance to have training on freelancing. I'm one of those. The workshop was for the dwellers of Jessore district. I took part of the training as I'm an inhabitant of Jessore district. The government arranges such workshops in several districts in the country.

Having trained, I filled out the virtual workplace agency form (oDesk.com). The trainers taught us practically how to fill up the form. The trainees, who brought their laptops at the training venue, filled up their forms on the spot. I had to fill up the form at my residence as I did not bring my laptop in the training place.

All the information that I wrote on the form is accurate. I took the marketplace's custom readiness test. For me, the test was hard because the questions were not familiar to my knowledge. I had to search for the answers. So, I took Google's help. The instructors who conducted the training sessions suggested us to take help from Google at the time of filling out the form. I just followed the suggestions.

In the form, the job seekers have their personal profiles. Personal information, specially, job oriented ones are needed to be inputted in the form. Every job seeker needs to give special attention on what job they are looking for during the application process. The job providers hire those who have experiences on the related fields. Only suitable candidates, who have experiences, would get the job. So, the job title is an important one for both the job seekers and the job providers. The title must be attracting in a way that relates the position. It may be simple, such as 'Looking for a job on creative writings'. In my title, I emphasized journalism oriented jobs.

I'm currently teaching at an English Medium school in Jessore, Bangladesh. I put up the information in my profile, too. My educational backgrounds were also given in the profile. I had so many trainings on journalism and creative writings. I simply put down the information in the profile without giving details. I did not say how many workshops I attended.

I took part in the U.S English Basic Skills and English Spelling Test (U.S Version) to improve my profile test scores. I did not do any homework for the tests. I think, what I did is not the proper process for taking part in such tests. Nobody is fulfilled in all the skills. It will be better for any job seeker to sit for any test if you're well-prepared. It will be an intelligent decision for the incumbents. It may be mentioned here that the required weight of anyone's personal profile is 100 percent. You have to have a great profile for having good jobs. You need to be careful about it. It is also important for job seekers to upload a simple and smart portrait on your profile.

In my profile, I gave my first name, last name and profile name. My user name is SR_Saif. Password selection is an important one too. You know that password protects you from theft. Your security could be at risk if it is visible to others. So, it should be strong. It would be best if your password consists of Alphanumeric and you should be able to memorize it. You can choose a name with three or four letters and a set of numbers with four to five digits as your password. For example, jenny1234. As you know, password is very much important for Internet users. So, don't use your cell phone numbers or your name in the password.

I want to add that my certificate name is Md Saifur Rahman. I love to use Saifur Rahman Saif while I am a writer or a journalist. Saifur Rahman is my first name and Saif is my last name. I completed a masters degree from a college under the National University of Bangladesh. I am excellent in Bangla and English both written and spoken.

As I chose creative writing as the medium of freelancing, I love to present myself to job providers as a journalist as well as a writer. At the time of bidding, I attach a sample of my writings with my application. The application in the bidding process is non-formal. No formality is used in the application.

It could be like this:

*Dear Hiring Manager,*

*I'm a creative writer and a journalist. Writing is my passion, profession and vision. I'm interested to work with you. I'll try to input my best performance if I'm hired.*

*Looking forward to hearing from you.*

I know that managers are very busy so I do not use too many words or long sentences in the job application. The outsourcing job providers are very much talented. They want to know only the key information about your professional background because they are efficient with the time they spend. So, all your communication should be job oriented. They do not have enough time to hear from you that you were a very good athlete at once or that you like to go fishing. Whilst you are applying for the job of software developer, you do not need to say that you are a good writer. They want to listen to you say that you are a good software developer. And, mention it if you have a strong background in a related field.

The freelancers who want to catch the first track of freelancing jobs should demand very little money for the position which they are applying for. Think about the requirements of the job providers before applying. Apply only for those jobs that match with your job background. If you do not have any experience in the fields of freelancing jobs, don't be disheartened. There are so many jobs waiting for you. So, make sure you're prepared for freelancing jobs and apply then. I'm sure you'll get a lot of jobs. Remember that experience is a thing that needs to be achieved. Don't worry about who you are! Just be prepared regarding freelancing. A strong will power is needed to have online jobs.

## My First Day on the Job Hunt

After filling out the oDesk.com form, I started searching for jobs. I tried very hard but failed to get any job in the first few days. At first I thought that I might not get any job at all. But I did not lose hope. Time came and I got a job. It was not an easy task. The job provider told me to write research papers on selected subjects. He told me to prepare five research projects within 24 hours. I was not familiar with such a type of work. I tried to write something. I couldn't even sleep. Out of the five, I completed three in one night. But I could not fulfill the demands of the job provider. He told me to search for the topic. Google helped me find it and I also watched videos for the research. Then the job provider told me that I was correct. I smiled. I became more confident in my skills.

## Great Employers are Out There

Then I got another job with a very cooperative lady. She responded to my queries right away. I wanted to work with her for a long time. But she ended my contract. She also assured me that she will hire me again in the future.

That client paid me on completion of every topic. After sending the money, she wanted to know whether I got the money. I'm still in search for a job with an employer like her.

## Conquering the Fear of Virtual Office Jobs

For getting jobs, I apply to positions that match my ability and my quality. I don't apply for jobs that are not familiar to me. I will definitely ask questions to the job provider just to make sure if it is new to me. One job was writing research on selected topics. It was obviously familiar to my skills. The thing that was not familiar to me is to download a video and then do research on that. I was told to finish research on various topics and watch videos. I had to write a minimum of 750 words for a single topic. It was completely a research job. However, I was able to overcome the job challenges that were seemingly unfamiliar to me.

For the job seekers, I wish to say that my first job was hard for me. I failed to realize it at the very beginning. Since I was a first-timer, tension mounted my mind. The tension I bore in my mind in doing my first online job is a part of human character.

Please note that while you are at the initial stage of online jobs, you'll demand a minimum per hour charge. It can be $2 or less keeping in mind that there are a lot of job seekers who want jobs by hook or by crook. You are one of them. So, at the time of bidding your demand should not cross those who are on the queue. I think having the first job is tougher than that off others so keep that in mind when bidding.

After getting jobs, you may need to fill out a form to make sure you get your money. Before filling out the forms, you may need to go to your bank and collect the SWIFT code. SWIFT code is needed for getting payments directly to your bank account. Wire payment system make it easy for freelancers to get money. For the citizens of America, freelancers usually need to fill out a tax payment form. The outsiders do not usually need it.

Freelancers from Bangladesh and many other countries are using wire transfer facilities for receiving payment. As I observed, oDesk is the only agency that brought wire transfer facilities for Bangladeshi freelancers at the time of this writing. Through this system, freelancers from Bangladesh are getting money directly in favor of their bank accounts.

Anyone who wants to make himself or herself a good freelancer needs to be a client of oDesk although oDesk is not the only agency that provides jobs. I suggest the job seekers to be the client of oDesk because it is reliable and service —oriented.

Please keep it in mind that online clients and jobs will chase after you if you are a good freelancer. And turning you as a good freelancer is labor-oriented. If you labor for online jobs, you'll be experienced. And the job providers seek a man or woman who has experience. I was not experienced; the others were not at the beginning of their online careers either. And if you do not yet have experience, do not worry. You can become an experienced freelancer in the future.

*Be faithful and confident, we shall overcome someday.*

**Saifur Rahman Saif**
*I'm a native Bangladeshi and a resident of Jessore district.*

*For more information about this contributor, view the Resources section at the end of this book.*

# Mind Games

*Noori never thought getting a job online is very convenient. It's like you could be your own boss at home. Thanks to her sister who introduced her to freelance work.*

*Story by Noori Shaikh*

Autobiography:

Hi guys my name is Maria Sh, I'm a student of medicine. Three months ago I was suffering from a financial crisis. Since I'm studying, I can't work and I'm having trouble managing my time.

My sister is a software engineer so she has a lot of knowledge about Information Technology and related fields. One day I went to a conference in the Marriot Hotel in Karachi, Pakistan. I heard about the online work, but I didn't take much interest in it until my sister started working on oDesk. She became a successful freelancer in just one month.

Now she advised me to apply into virtual workplaces as well so I created a profile right away. I applied in lots of data entry positions but didn't get any jobs. Instead, I applied for article writing since I'm good at it. I then got a response right away and I was so happy.

Let's take a look at my online work profile:

*Name: Noor-e-Hrum*

*City: Karachi*

*Country: Pakistan*

*Title: data entry, online teacher, content writing, article writing, web research, online GIT consultant*

*Qualification: BEMS for 3 years and I'm good at multi-tasking.*

My first winning job is in the article writing position and they paid me $5 for it. Well, I don't have any advertising skills. But now I'm doing adult content writing and it's going great.

Well it's a great job without any bosses around. I advise this job to those who want to make money without getting a headache.

*Noori Shaikh*
*freelancing - 6 months*
*Karachi, Pakistan*

*For more information about this contributor, view the Resources section at the end of this book.*

# Inch by Inch Closer

*Monjour is an expert in building web-based applications.*

*One day he decided, "instead of always logging into Facebook, I might as well go to oDesk.com and be productive and earn good money."*

*Story by Monjur Ahmed*

Biography:

My name is Monjur Ahmed from Dhaka, Bangladesh and this is the story of my freelancing career as an expert web based application developer. As a software engineer and system analyst with more than 5 years experience, I have started freelancing to be my own boss and to share my knowledge that I have achieved through my education and professional experience.

This is my story —the beginning of a dream to be successful in freelancing.

Creating a profile:

It was most important to create my profile once I created my freelancing account. I needed to have a profile that would reflect the true 'me'. Though creating a profile on a freelancing platform is straightforward as all the required sections are prompted to be filled, it takes a lot of care and precision.

At the time of creating my profile, it was very important for me to choose the correct words to describe myself including my skill-set. Though it sounds easy, representing my true self is not obvious —it demands careful thought and proper wording to convey the message that I want to pass to the rest of the world.

My profile should be about what I really am so that the employers will be assured that they are hiring the right person. A very important aspect about the profile is not to leave it on total 'self certification'. I declare to be proficient on some tools and that is purely a self certification. So what is the way to justify my claimed expertise? Thanks to the certification tests that are provided by outsourcing platforms, I proved my skills. By passing the tests, I established my claim of being an expert on the tools I have mentioned in my profile. But taking the test needs careful planning.

Taking Skill Tests

As a software engineer and web based application developer, the tests that I need to pass are the ones related to my field. The following three aspects came into consideration when I was looking for new jobs. I wanted to ensure by the tests I take, that these important aspects are covered.

I am communicative and I have presentation skills which would let the employer know I am proficient in keeping communication —to understand and to be understood. English language tests were important for this aspect.

I am skillful on the set of tools I have claimed in my profile. Various exams on specific tools were necessary to be passed to establish my claim of being an expert on the tools I have specified in my profile.

I'm very good at managing my projects very well. I need to prove that I am well capable of understanding Information Technology projects since I'm well trained in the software development field. That is why I need to take the tests that are related to general management, product quality and other related topics.

So it is apparent from the above discussion that taking tests for a freelancer is very important as well as taking proper and relevant tests so that the employers know I am skillful to carry out the tasks successfully.

Profile and tests are also linked with the portfolio —the samples of my work in other words. There should be harmonization among all these three and they should complement each other. I have chosen the works that best describe my skills. The portfolio is a very effective means to present myself —as nothing is better than illustration to convey the message.

<u>Winning work:</u>

I had come across a lot of demotivating stories with some virtual workers having being refused on bidding jobs for a year which eventually ended in them giving up their career as a freelancer. Were I demotivated and disheartened with those stories? Most probably not otherwise I would not be writing this article! But the stories gave me one good indication even before I started knocking on the employers' doors to win a project. The lesson is —never be whimsical when bidding.

When I joined oDesk.com, I got my first interview in less than 24 hours. I did not get the job because my bid was too high. Like anyone else, it was my dream to get the first job order; yet I did not compromise on the price based on the fact that I cannot satisfy my client if I myself am not satisfied. So I do not bid just to get the order. I have a belief that everything has a threshold which may be subjective at times; quality is proportional to the time and effort given.

This belief makes me try to get only the projects where I am fully confident that I can serve the best quality. I believe this is a very motivating foundation for me and it's totally up to me to keep this foundation strong which will only be assured by satisfying my employers on an ongoing basis.

I consider every successful project to be another feather to my freelancing hat.

It is a crucial matter to make sure that I can convince my employer to trust that their project has been given to the right person. To convince the employers and to subsequently get the job, there is no elixir except love and care. I feel I need to love the work to give my full effort. In addition, I need to fully understand my employer's requirements. The secret lies in taking care of the employer's problem and to make it my problem. Then to deal with love and care, to know all about it so that the employer's requirements are fully satisfied by my work without missing anything. As a software engineer, I always adopt an epistemological approach towards system analysis.

To win at job seeking, I believe the cover letter plays a very important role. Every cover letter needs to be unique as every single project is unique. Custom tailored cover letters show my care for the job I am applying to.

Delivering the Work:

Winning the work is just the start. Once I get an order, I need to make proper planning for the whole project. I like to work in a structured way and so I take control of project planning and management software. Then I can manage and keep track of the schedule and resource allocation as well as other aspects of my project.

It is very important to keep regular communication with the employer and to give updates on the work, preferably on a daily basis. I personally follow what we the software engineers call JAD (Joint Application Development) approach in my projects where I ensure a high involvement of my employer when the project goes on. It helps to make sure for both me and my employer that the right thing is being developed. Thus, delivering the work is a gradual process with every single bit of update.

Getting paid:

I believe all payments should be done through the outsourcing platform. For example, I like to get paid only through the outsourcing platform because I find it to be secure.

Advertising and Networking

I contribute a significant amount of time on freelancing platforms —
especially on oDesk where I apply to more and more projects (within
my job application quota, of course) and it helps me to build my profile
even if I am not awarded by the project.

People do Facebook all the time and I do oDesk! I love to use all my
time on oDesk —it is fun, creative and there is a lot to learn just by
browsing. It gives me the feeling of achievement when I take a test and
get a good grade. I see the creative side of being a freelancer and I know
I still have to go a long way. I believe I can make it if I have the love and
care —for me and for my work.

In the future, I plan to expand my business online and focus on creative tasks where I can tap into my passion.

*Monjour Ahmed*
*Freelancer*
*Dhaka, Bangladesh*

*For more information about this contributor, view the Resources section at the end of this book.*

# Far from Fetch

*Mirijed is a young, ambitious guy who takes challenges positively and is very good at developing strategies for himself and his employers.*

I am a young ambitious guy who takes challenges positively and undertakes viable initiatives to counter day-to-day drawbacks and develop strategies to make ends meet. In the recent past I have been able to secure various job titles as a catalyst to my career development.

My job title in oDesk is Customer Service Representative. Basically, I carry out market research on different customer queries. Under this job specification I seek to optimize on the customer satisfaction level. It's only under this we are able to optimize profits on company undertakings.

Another freelance job title I have is Email handler. Under this job title I undertake various tasks; email response, copy and pasting emails to Microsoft Excel and dealing with spam emails.

Thirdly, I am a certified public accountant by profession. I compute companies end-of-period balance sheets including profit and loss accounts. I also compute corporation taxes and dividends to both preferential and ordinary shareholders.

The last job title I have is Data entry Manager. I fetch data from the internet and other websites and feed it into Microsoft Excel.

MY EDUCATION AND PERSONAL INTERESTS

I am student in the university undertaking a degree in purchasing and supplies management. In addition to that I have certifications as a certified public accountant from the Visions Institute of Professionals. Finally, I also took a course in Computer Studies. Using this experience, I familiarized myself with areas like spreadsheets, databases and Microsoft PowerPoint. On September 23rd I attended an entrepreneur conference.

My personal interests include: writing articles, playing basketball, playing table tennis and making friends both locally and abroad.

I created my profile ranging from three to four months ago. Basically I was introduced to outsource work by a friend of mine. I filled in all my particulars as required of me. It was a simple task for me as I had all details with me and certifications. In addition, I undertook several tests to prove that I have the stated skills.

Generally, I present myself as a qualified contractor to my employers and along with that is an attachment of my certifications and qualifications.

To advertise my skills to my employers, I undertake relevant skill tests and make sure that I achieve a high feedback scores from completed jobs that will improve my profile.

WINNING WORK

One thing that will make an employer choose you over other qualified contractors is how you quote a bid on project. Basically I will look at the task to be assigned to me and quote a fair bid on a project.

It would unreasonable to quote a high price on a small project which will require minimal time to complete it. I also browse through clients' profiles to see whether they are reliable in terms of payment schedules regarding past projects undertaken by various contractors.

DELIVERING THE WORK

I schedule myself to work for at least eight hours a day. As soon as I'm done with a piece of work I communicate it to my client and submit it promptly without any delay. I also submit reports to my employer on how far I am with the job. This helps the employer gain confidence in you and looks forward to working with you once more. Basically, I deliver work done through my personal email for the employer to examine.

## GETTING PAID

Generally, I prefer payments through Skrill or Wire Transfers. I consider these two the best payments as there are no delays. My employers pay me depending on the work done. If my employer approves my work, then I will receive payments as agreed.

On average I get seventy five to one hundred and fifty dollars a week depending on tasks completed that week. I am paid for jobs like email response handling, data entry, customer service and book keeping.

## ADVERTISING INFORMATION

I market my skills by listing the various jobs I have completed and giving a good client feedback. To make sure employers know who I am, I have verified my account by providing a scanned representation of my National Identity Card and Bank Statement.

I am Mirijed Muruthi. I currently reside in Nairobi City, Kenya.

*Mirijed Muruthi*
*Nairobi City, Kenya*

*For more information about this contributor, view the Resources section at the end of this book.*

# Absence of the Corporate Bliss

*Kim thinks freelancing requires commitment.*

*She was able to find a way to love what she's doing while earning at the same time.*

*Story by Kim Cruea*

The Joys, Woes, and In Betweens of Freelancing

Kim Cruea—Author of nine books, Freelance Writer since 2007.

If you enjoy writing, illustrating, designing stationary, or have a knack for web design, then becoming a freelancer might be a great option for you. Becoming a freelancer wasn't my initial goal, however, a few twists and turns seemingly landed me in this position and now I love it—most of the time.

My experience in freelancing has covered ghostwriting, rewriting, editing, screenwriting, scripts, press releases, articles, and completing childrens' books (illustrating a few as well). Freelancing anything requires commitment, know how, panic and joy. Each talent you possess is marketable, but the competition is tough. While your work might be worth $50 per hour, there are people with the same quality who are willing to do it for $3/hour. Most cannot survive on $3, so choosing your jobs will be tricky.

As a freelancer I have learned more about my best skills and my 'not-so-great' skills. While I know I can cartoon, there are incredible artists out there I wouldn't be able to compete with. Recognizing your specialty is a great place to start. Freelancing covers so many areas; deciding which area is best for you primarily comes down to knowing your own personal strengths and weaknesses.

The types of freelancing can cover technical skills (web design), art skills (Photoshop, hand art, photography, digital art, cartooning, graphic art etc.), research (legal, business), and writing (ghost writing, articles, blogs, e-books, reviews, etc.).

Even if you are able to do ALL of these, it's not a bad idea to focus on the areas you excel. That is because working with your talent will win client approval and reviews; thus bringing you new clients. Even if you can write an article, if you're not passionate with it, it may show in your work.

My work began just over five years ago when my first book got published. Soon afterwards, someone asked me to do some creative writing work for them and then I received a monetary reward for the work done. It was then that I decided that I would explore the world of freelance.

The journey wasn't immediately fruitful. In fact, there were periods when the work was less lucrative and my family struggled to make ends meet. Then, there were times when the financial rewards were amazing. Quickly burned due to the 'recovery' period from previous work drought, but in following this pattern, I learned how to juggle it better.

In the end, freelance work became a full time job, but I supplemented the income with a part time —out of the house job. A regular offline income I could count on alleviated some of the stress of the online job.

Some of the joys of freelancing have been:

- Good pay (sometimes)

- Meeting amazingly interesting and diverse individuals, hearing unusual stories, interviewing legends, and doing what I already love to do.

- Being —somewhat —in control of what projects I do, when I do them, and what time of the day I work on them.

The downfalls of freelancing have been:

- The challenge of finding your next job.

- The challenge of collecting payment.

- Dealing with interruptions—there are many people who don't understand the concept of self-employment. Being able to manage interruptions can be tricky, but is a necessary part of the job. Especially when you are in need of quiet in a house full of children, all demanding your attention. It wasn't easy juggling the two, but finding time slots to write and time slots to clean or play with kids, and make meals took much effort.

Finding a way to make money, doing what you love is wonderful, but knowing that "WONDERFUL" will be met with adversities and challenges is an important reality to grasp. It won't be easy, but it will definitely have its rewards. If you can find a time and place to do your work efficiently then you should do it. Nothing brings you more satisfaction then completing a job for your client and having them gleaming with gratitude upon completion.

Whether you decide to write, draw, or design web pages; being happy with yourself will take you ¾ of the way. The other ¼ is simply the need to know that keeping your clients happy is the best and only way to ensure freelancing survival.

*Kim Cruea*
*Freelancer since fall 2007*
*Barrie, Ontario Canada*

*For more information about this contributor, view the Resources section at the end of this book.*

# Fame and Shame

*Joanna earns money while doing her favorite things – reading and writing.*

*Story by Joanna Paula Cailas*

## BIOGRAPHY

I'm Joanna Paula L. Cailas. I live in Marilao, Bulacan in the Philippines. I'm a freelance writer and editor. You can append all other titles related to writing and editing here. Saying I read a lot is an understatement. I gobble everything from medicine inserts and website disclaimers to flash fiction and whole sagas that won't be done until perhaps I'm forty. Being a voracious reader led to writing, and writing led to editing as I learned more and more about the craft. Friends from the US and the UK have commented on my almost-scary command of their native language. I tell them I only get my expertise from my constant exposure to English. I try to read more Filipino these days, to balance my knowledge and to shake off a tiny feeling of disloyalty.

I'm profoundly deaf, a side-effect of contracting meningitis when I was thirteen, so I spend my days reading and writing. And now, after signing up for freelance work, I actually earn money while doing my favorite things. Awesome!

I love Victoriana—and most historical eras, really—quiz shows, fashion (the bulk of my current jobs are in this field), YA novels, memoirs and dogs. I've seen several job postings that match these interests, and they put the beauty and excitement in freelancing for me.

One of our family friends, Aunt Marj, had mentioned oDesk to me years before. But I've come across many 'freelancing' sites and they all promised jobs in exchange for money. So I ignored Aunt Marj's short text message.

And then my brother browsed oDesk a few weeks ago. The next morning, I was the one who was nearly done with my profile and absolutely addicted to the online skill tests.

With jobs demanding my time, I've also strangely shaken off my persistent case of writer's block. I actually have material to put to paper for my own novel now that I miss it every day. Absence does make the heart grow fonder.

## CREATING A PROFILE

I had both fun and jitters while creating my profile on oDesk and Elance. Seeing my published work again as others would view them was both gratifying and sort of frustrating—I was thinking, 'I want more! This is all I've got?' and 'Wow! I can't believe this piece of genius and wit came from me!' Kidding. But you know what they say about your creations being like your babies? It's true. And when I created my profile and portfolio, it was like putting my babies on display. Feelings of shyness and pride are normal, I suppose, and I felt them keenly.

There are tips all over the Internet about creating your profile, but I only saw them afterward when I was looking for tips on freelancing in general. While building my profile, I went with my gut instinct and just enumerated and described what I am very much able to deliver to potential clients.

I edited and revised my taglines and description of services or job goals several times. I wanted my confidence and comfort with my line of work to shine through. At the same time, I had to decide whether or not to include certain keywords there. In the end, I decided my skill is best displayed with subtlety and class rather than clunky directness. Even SEO principles say that good content would trump focusing on keywords anytime.

As I've mentioned above, I was quite enamored with the tests. I loved the spelling and vocabulary tests. The grammar tests, not so much. Maybe because I'm only in the top thirty percent in those instead of the top ten or twenty? Haha. I find that grammar is like algebra. You don't really apply all those terminologies and formulas, or at least, you're not aware of doing so as you go along. I recognize both good and bad paragraphs and sentences when I see them, but I can't pinpoint exactly why they're wrong and what this clause or that one is called. I just know when they don't read right. I change that, and the client is satisfied. Where's grammar there? Some people can spout off grammar terms and rules and still write terribly anyway. One simply absorbs the rules and nuances of the language through lots of reading.

## WINNING WORK

I quite dislike it when the clients make us quote. Some clients on Elance would put 'Not Sure' on their budgets. And then they decline bids that are 'too high'. I've learned to keep my bid inside the client's budget, if a budget is specified. When they're not sure, I quote several standard rates. For example, editorial rates have standard amounts in the professional world. I follow that with a discount. Ten to twelve dollars for comprehensive cleanup and critique. Five dollars for touch ups on punctuation and mechanics and the like.

Whether or not my quote includes or excludes oDesk or Elance fees, I decide by how much I'd love to do the work involved. I'm willing to lower my pay for my favorite project types.

In my cover letters, I always show that I've understood all the relevant details cited in the job posting. Delivery times are particularly important alongside the assurance that you can deliver within deadline without compromising on the thoroughness and quality of the work.

## DELIVERING THE WORK

My dad and mom advised me to manage my time well. There are also tips all over the internet on allotting time to certain jobs on certain hours or certain days. My own rule is that I work when I'm free and I work on what's most urgent, like fulfilling quotas.

As for the submission, I use the Rich Text Format (.rtf) for documents I compose myself. It's the most universal document type that can be opened on any machine of any age. If the client sends a document in .docx, I keep to that format whenever I can. If they ask for PDF, I deliver in PDF.

GETTING PAID

Clients pay through oDesk or Elance, and so far, my clients have all been prompt in their payments. The first day after finishing building my profile and portfolio on oDesk is also the day I won my first job. The client immediately forwarded the upfront payment I've asked for and the thrill this gave me almost knocked me over. It was great.

I get different amounts of income from my hourly and fixed-price jobs. Anywhere from $2 for precision editing of snippets of copy for websites, to over $100 for bigger proofreading jobs.

As of the time of this submission, I've had one experience with a probable scammer. The client invited me to the job. My first invitation. Very flattering. The client had no feedback or payment history, but so did some of my earlier clients who were perfectly legitimate. Naturally, I accepted the candidacy and wrote the 300-word keyword article asked for.

Shortly after submission, the client suddenly canceled my candidacy and said I wasn't qualified after all.

Either I really messed up, or that client got several free articles from every one he invited. Have you had a similar encounter? What can we do? Clients are within their rights to ask for sample articles. Contractors just starting up can't simply decline every job invitation from clients with no records. It's an impasse.

On Marketing My Profile

I haven't marketed my skills anywhere else aside from oDesk and Elance. But I make sure my profile is concise and catchy, highlighting my skills and providing proof of those skills.

To make sure employers remember me, I rename all documents with the title of the work and my name. And of course, I have a professional email with my actual name, and my signature on it contains my full name, job title and email addresses. These are small efforts towards advertising your services, but they work.

*Joanna Paula Cailas*
*Marilao, Bulacan Philippines*

*For more information about this contributor, view the Resources section at the end of this book.*

# Something New

*Charles likes portfolios. He thinks one of the key things that distinguish an application from a freelance profile is the need for a well-stocked and up-to-date portfolio.*

## BIOGRAPHY

Charles Franklin is a freelance writer, researcher, and virtual assistant with over 11 years of experience in libraries, customer service, and almost everything in between. His current writing specialties are employment, business, social networking, philosophy, education and religion. He holds an Associate Degree in Social Science Education along with over 25 hours of coursework in psychology, sociology, and social work. He also attended Augusta State University and almost completed a Bachelor of Social Work, but found that the Universe had other plans for him.

Charles is a "green" learning addict, online social advocate and Nerd Fitness Rebel who is looking to forge in a new path in his family's legacy. In addition to the above services, he also offers pro-bono grant writing, content writing, volunteer administration and research services for selected non-profits in the environment, cultural and health fields. When he is not writing, completing job proposals, running family errands, he enjoys laughing, watching sports, pretending to do martial arts and reading. Beside all of that, he is also a poet-in-training who writes haiku and free-verse poetry in mythology, spirituality and nature. He has worked for Odesk, Textbroker, ContentBLVD, Blogmutt, Article Document and other private individuals and corporations. He has been published in the Augusta State University Sandhills Literary Magazine and Yahoo Voices Contributor Network.

## CREATING A PROFILE

Before I became serious about freelancing, I approached my freelance profile like a job application. I filled out the required parts and expected employers to read through my achievements as evidence of my ability to work. I quickly came to realize that this will not work on a freelancing profile. One of the key things that distinguish an application from a freelance profile is the need for a well-stocked and up-to-date portfolio of assessments and work samples.

Employers who hire for on-site jobs can complete in-person interviews and use other methods to attempt to narrow down their candidate list to the most suitable candidate. Employers who hire virtual workers or online freelancers are in a more precarious position because they lack the safeguards typically offered to employers from face-to-face meetings.

To compensate for this, employers who use freelancers often require evidence of work you have done before and assessments that show you have the initiative and consideration necessary to do the job. When I shifted to full-time freelance work, I improved my freelance profile by doing two things.

First, I reviewed the profile of well-established freelancers in my fields of interest (writing and administrative support). This provided guidance on some of the typical work samples, assessments and certifications needed to excel in my field. Second, I included work samples and assessments to match every area that I was offering services in. This allowed employers to see that I know how to market myself. I update and review all of my portfolio work on a regular basis to ensure that I have the best work and also the highest credentials I can offer at the time. I advertise updates to my portfolio pieces through my social networks (such as Twitter and LinkedIn) to keep my network of contacts updated on my projects. It sounds like a lot of work, but when you hear from an employer (especially a well-paying one) that is really impressed with your portfolio, it is all worth it.

WINNING WORK

I currently work on both bidding and non-bidding projects. Since I am still new to online freelance, I am currently focusing on non-bidding projects to ensure an adequate income supply as well as a steady supply of portfolio pieces. When I bid on a project, I take into consideration three things:

- Number of freelancers applying for the project

- My experience and interest in the project

- Time-frame and workload of the project

Since I am still a new online freelancer, my quotes are lower than I normally would charge. This is because I know employers are on a budget and that if I work well, I can get repeat clients. Repeat clients are a goldmine in the world of freelancing. This actually happened with my second online job. I bid a little lower than normal, but delivered the end product quickly. When I did so, I was instantly hired for another project and another, until I surpassed the amount I would have originally charged. I would not recommend this strategy for all project bids, because it can seem to devalue your labor. This strategy does work good; however when you have a lot of freelancers applying for the job (if you know this in advance).

For project bids, where I have significant experience and interest, I will bid at the client's suggested price or slightly above to demonstrate my confidence in my abilities. I also use that strategy for jobs that will require significant workload. From there, it's a matter of demonstrating that ability through ensuring my portfolio materials (along with other requirements) match the employer's needs as closely as possible. I have a template for job bidding, but it is highly customizable, so that I can create a highly personal cover letter with work samples. After that, I keep up with job applications and follow up with clients regularly. One tip I have recently learned that has recently helped me concerns the e-mail subject line. The way you craft your subject line in an e-mail to a prospective client can influence whether they open your e-mail. Once you pass that hurdle, you've much closer to getting the employer's attention.

## DELIVERING THE WORK

One of the greatest things about freelance work is the variety of work (and workloads) that can happen from day to day and sometimes hour to hour. When I first started freelancing, I had a hard time prioritizing projects because I was eager to take on anything. This often led to long nights and even longer mornings. As I have gotten more used to the workload and a list of reliable clients, I am better able to prioritize. Right now, I begin work around 7am after meditation and getting something to eat. I check my e-mail for any updates to any of the projects I have applied to (adding them to my "Must-Do-Today" List) and begin working on my priorities. During lunch or during breaks, I check my e-mail (updating as needed); otherwise, I work on my selected work projects for the day and I'm done. For big projects require more than a day's work, I will send a work update letting my client know how much I achieved that day. Most of the time this will get done quite early, allowing a lot of free time to rest or market myself some time. Every once in a while, I may have to pull a late-nighter to get things done, but this is happening less and less often.

The other good thing about freelance work is the extremely low overhead and equipment needed to do the job. All of my clients are online; therefore all I need is word-processing software and Internet access for most clients. For some customer service jobs, I do need a headset and use of the second line. Otherwise, everything I need to complete a job is on my laptop.

## GETTING PAID

As mentioned above, all of my work is done online, so the predominant method of pay is online through direct deposit or PayPal. For clients that pay directly through PayPal, the amount and frequency of pay varies. For clients that pay through a third party, like Odesk, Guru, or Elance, the pay usually comes around every Thursday or Friday or some other regular pattern. I only have one or two clients that pay by check.

For writing jobs, the pay varies from $1 to $40 for articles and for blog postings around 400-800 words. The variety is really dependent on your writing skill, deadline date, and subject matter. For customer service jobs, the pay usually runs between $8 and $13 an hour. Research jobs range from $20 to $100 per project or per hour. Transcription jobs start off low, but can climb up to $10 for 30-40 minutes and sometimes it goes even higher than  that depending.

ADVERTISING INFORMATION

When it comes to marketing and advertising, whenever I'm working I'm always looking for an opportunity to find clients. This is a big mind-shift from my days as an employee, when I became rather lazy with my portfolio and marketing myself. As a freelancer, I advertise through a lot of venues: social networking, word of mouth, listing myself on freelancing web-sites, interacting on freelancing and work at home blogs and forums, and providing free or reduced cost services to non-profits. Once I have completed the project, I send an e-mail to confirm everything is finished, confirm payment details and to evaluate my service. I regularly check on these clients by e-mail and phone to confirm their details and to see if there are any areas I can assist them with. If I see an area that I can assist with in any venue, I offer my e-mail and phone number to follow up.

I am in the process of building a blog and website to further advertise my skills and achievements to prospective clients.

*Charles Franklin*
*Atlanta, GA*

*For more information about this contributor, view the Resources section at the end of this book.*

# Stages of Trials

*Ali was an average student during his school life. He struggled to overcome his fears. He lived up to others' expectations before finally developing into a self-made person with vision and motive.*

My name is Syed Aun Ali Jafri. I was born in Dubai, but, a citizen of
Pakistan, as my parents are Pakistani. I spent my childhood in Dubai,
where I studied in a Cambridge board system.

When I was fourteen, the world around me started to fall apart. I had to
live through a lot of crisis and at times all by myself. In those moments,
I picked up my pen and scribbled the papers with my thoughts. Those
thoughts turned into poems and stories. Gradually, I let the crumbling
world out of my head and explored the world inside me. When I did
that, I found a writer within me. I decided to complete my education
and since school was not an option, I studied privately. Who knew it
was all happening for my own benefit.

While I studied privately for the Cambridge exams, I showed my
English teacher, who loved literature, a few of my poems for correction.
She said I was a 'poet in-the-making'. She believed I had the aptitude to
score high in English Literature and with just two months for the exams
to start, I decided to add English Literature to my list of subjects.

Focusing mostly on Literature, I passed the next two months learning
about the best subject I've ever come across. To me, Literature was the
most interesting subject. Anyhow, with the guidance of my teacher, I
appeared for the exam well prepared.

By the blessing of God almighty, I achieved an A* in Literature. It was
the single greatest moment I had in those years of hardships and
struggle, and I had to thank my teacher for it.

As the months passed by, I polished my talent and before I knew it, I
was writing for several clients at a time to support my family. I was only
seventeen when I took the responsibility to help my family in that hard
time. Obviously, my family played a big part in it by encouraging me
every step of the way and on top of it all, God was the biggest reason for
my success. The way my proposals were accepted was unbelievable. One

minute, my family and I discussed about the shortage of money and the next thing I knew was that I had 1 new message in my Gmail account and it was from a client on oDesk.com.

How I Got Into Online Contracting

When I got accepted in Murdoch University, the only thing keeping me out was the fees. We could not afford the fees, hence I had to stay at home. Watching me write stories as time passes, my cousin introduced me to an online website called 'oDesk'. He believed I had the potential to work as a freelance writer so he suggested that I should check it out.

I made an oDesk account and what I did first was to improve my profile. I made it look professional going with the title (Fiction writer/Creative writer/Article writer/ Music artist) and then appeared for a few tests. Completing the tests related to my field had a great impact on my job applications, as the clients gauged my English skills by checking my scores. Moreover, I displayed a decent profile picture, letting the clients know that I was a serious worker.

At first, I kept my hourly rate at $2/hr. This helped me in getting a quick start in the working business and the vital experience, which I needed the most. But, to get the jobs I had to convince the clients first that I was the right candidate for them. Without a good cover letter, most clients do not bother checking the contractor's profile. Hence, I read a sample on how to write a good cover letter on oDesk. By reading that, I got a better idea on setting the tone of the letter. While keeping it professional, I also managed to display my heart on the cover letters. I displayed my talents and proved to the clients that I have the skills to complete the required tasks. I provided them with samples of my work and since I worked as a creative writer, I ignited my creative spark in it.

Adding items in the portfolio increased the value of my profile even further. I added my poetry group 'Exploring My Heart' in the portfolio and some of my other writings.

By taking the U.S English spelling test, I answered most of the client's questions before hand, as clients frequently stress on applicants spelling skills. In addition, I entered a creative writing and English vocabulary test. By achieving a good score in all three of them, I set a strong base for my future.

Obviously, the tests required a certain amount of preparation at first. And, since I had no idea how hard they were going to be, I entered for the easiest one first. Before giving the test, I skimmed through the syllabus. I had to do some research on the Internet, as I was not familiar with some of the portion. Anyhow, I managed to complete it long before the timer stopped. The result immediately came out and I was delighted with my score.

Convincing the Clients

Showing off your skills without sounding too proud is a tough task. In the beginning, I wondered if I should brag about my skills or not. In my first few cover letters, I opted not to brag much.

Since, I am a creative writer; I ignored the prior thoughts and came up with a brilliant idea. I decided to 'express' my skills. Like they tell you in fiction writing courses 'show not tell', I improvised this technique in my cover letters.

The experiment worked very well. I received invitations for job interviews. But, the hardest part for me in the beginning was to get the first job. At times, I was shortlisted by the client, only to see a day later that my job offer had been declined.

Once I made the perfect profile, I had difficulty convincing the employers that I could do the job. That's the part where I had to display my confidence and flamboyance. However, each time the employers invited me to interviews and asked me questions about my work experience, I tried to dodge the bullet by being abrupt and unconvincing.

It took me about a month to get my first job and I started on only $1.50 per 5 articles. I had to work hard to earn that little amount, but, it was worth it. The amount of experience I gained; the increase in knowledge was remarkable. I learned about writing articles more than I ever did before. I learned new words, new places, new information and that's what kept me going. My parents said "Son, the start is always tough. Once you get your foot into the business world, it'll all run smoothly." With their prayers and words of inspiration, I worked on that job with all my heart. In the mean time, I kept applying for other jobs as well. ODesk has a quota of 20 applications at a time and so I submitted my proposals at different job postings.

Within a week's time, I received a reply from an employer. The joy that brought to my heart when I saw a red circle in my inbox was unbelievable. I had applied for a sports news writing position and the employer liked my cover letter. I have always been a big fan of sports and so I decided to go for it. In my job interview, I was confident and relaxed. I answered all the questions accordingly and to the point. I was sure that I had got it. However, I did not receive any new messages from him in four days. At first, I thought that he must have selected someone else. But, there was no notification about the job being closed. So, I composed a message stating if I had the job or not.

The next day, when I opened my Gmail account, I had one new message and it was from him. I was hired for the news writing post. He asked for my contact details and I shared my Skype details with him. We discussed about the payment and the job. I had several questions regarding the news posts, which I properly pointed out to him.

Work Time

Once I started the job, I took it very seriously. I respected the client's demands and made sure I produced top quality news posts every day. Since the workload was doubled, I resigned from my first job and focused completely on this one.

Before starting the work, I created a new folder in my job file. I labeled it with 'news writing' and started creating documents there. I always double-checked my work before sending it to the client, making sure it was error free and perfect. Moreover, I cleared my doubts with him regularly, keeping in touch all the time.

During the first few days, I made a few errors while posting the news on Wordpress. Plus, I made some formatting errors, which continued for over a week. Since, I accepted my mistakes and worked on them, the client remained satisfied and constantly encouraged me. He appreciated my writing skills and said I just needed to work on my Wordpress skills.

Over time, I learned how to handle Wordpress. In addition, I formatted the documents according to his demands, as I noted down all of his instructions in a WordPad file under the name 'Instruction manual'. Each time, I completed a post, I checked if the formatting was done accordingly.

The client and I were pleased as the work was running smoothly. The job continued for over a month and then the project was completed, thereby ending the contract. After ending the contract on great terms, I was ready for another job. With a five-star feedback, my chances of getting another job were looking good.

Getting job in the field of creative writing requires sheer talent and a great deal of confidence. Moreover, believing in yourself is vital. After writing several samples for a dozen job posts, without receiving any replies, I lived a brief moment of bleakness. That feeling almost pushed me away from writing another sample for a job post. But, I closed my eyes and conversed with my God and I found peace.

Few days later, I browsed through the list of new jobs and applied for a short stories ghostwriting post. Quickly, I composed a sample short story on Microsoft Word and attached it with my cover letter.

The red circle on my email inbox lifted my heart again. It was for the short stories post and the client said that she liked my sample and was looking forward to work with me. Subsequently, she added me on Skype and discussed the details. She asked me if I could submit a short story in every five days. I gazed at the screen blankly as it was a hard task creating and completing a 4000 plus words story in just five days and then start another one. But, then a feeling ran over my body and it assured me that I could do it. Without delaying any longer, I agreed to her terms and started the assignment.

It turned out that completing a story in five days was not difficult. In fact, I completed them a day before the deadline. So, I planned my schedule with four days of work and one day of rest.

Continuing the routine for over a month, the client ultimately changed the genre. The new genre (Mystery and Sci-Fiction) was new to me. I had never written a story on this topic before. Still, I gladly accepted to take the work.

For the first two days, I researched everything there was to know about this Genre. I read a couple of short stories related to it, before finally watching the picture inside my head. First, I create the story in my mind. Then, I create an outline and the character sketches.

After pulling a couple of all-nighters, I managed to submit the story a few hours before the deadline. I submitted the document to her. Then, the client sent it for checking and after a day of chills, I finally came to know that the story was approved.

<u>Organizing and Earnings</u>

When I started as a freelance writer, working on a slow computer was difficult and time consuming. So, I bought a mini-laptop with my first pay. It became easier for me to organize my files and keep work separate from other files.

The bigger question was, 'how well did I organize my work and life?' Well, at first I had a tough time juggling life and work. Mainly because, I had yet to make an impact in the freelance world and the start is always the hardest. At times, I had to skip family programs to complete work assignments. It had an impact on my social life, until I figured out a way to manage my life.

Writing has always been my passion and I thought why it should be any different while working. So, as my mom said "don't pressure yourself. Take it easy." I obeyed her words and stopped pressurizing myself too much. I stopped forcing myself to work all the time. Instead, I refreshed myself so I could then work with full attention. This way, I was able to complete the same number of assignments in half the working time. Furthermore, I planned a schedule wherein my working hours were early; hence, I had more time to spend with my family and friends.

Another thing I learned from my freelance experience is that it is best to work on a single job at a time. Unless, the job is simple and less time-consuming, there is no need to work on multiple jobs at a time.

The earnings are fairly normal in the freelance writing world. The clients I worked with usually had a flat-fee. I received the payment in my oDesk account once the work I submitted was approved.

Normally, I earned $20 per short story and $80 for a Novella. The prices varied from client to client, but, usually they were around these numbers.

Furthermore, I earned up to $2.50 per article, thereby, making around $250 per month.

This is a substantial sum that I was able to build on. For others who are interested in working like this, just remember that you can grow your business over time.

In my opinion, freelancing has been a great way to gain experience. Not only did I practice my writing skills, I also learned how to deal with people in the business world. Even though, the pay might not be as high as most expect, it is still a great experience.

*Ali Jafri*
*Lahore, Pakistan*

*For more information about this contributor, view the Resources section at the end of this book.*

# Conclusion

You have just peeked into the mind of successful international freelancers. It is our desire to communicate with you the passion of these freelancers so that you will be inspired to pursue your own dream as an accomplished professional freelancer.

There were many things that the freelancers shared in common which seemed to lead them to success.

**Communication, Passion, Inspiration**

All the freelancers of this edition worked with unbridled communication, unstoppable passion and an inspired life.

*Communication*

Communication is a tool for workplace harmony. It facilitates understanding among people and nations. More than harmony, communication has facilitated global progress, particularly through information technology.

Business operations have become seamless. Just like our online freelancers, they deliver their services through the Internet. Physical distance has been virtually shortened and communication between workers and employers are real-time, 24 hours per day, 365 days a year.

*Passion*

The passionate freelancer usually gets the job more than the one whose passion cannot be felt by the prospective client. Passion is an intense emotion compelling feeling, enthusiasm, or desire for something. Clients want the freelancers to truly care about the job and passion is an easy way to measure that commitment.

*Inspiration*

We pursued these freelancers because of the diverse experience each went through just so they can earn additional income, just so they could express their sentiments, and so that they could help others by sharing personal stories.

Remember the accounts of some of them? The first red notification mark is always the most exciting, though clients businesses tinged with a bit of apprehension. The notification brings only one of two reports: you have been hired, or you have been declined!

For every declined application, these freelancers moved on. Remember *Saifur*? Faith and confidence were his advice, but he sings you "shall overcome someday..." We know he did.

Real or virtual, the freelance professional is this generation's focus. No matter if you are in the United States working for a business in Asia, or if you are in the Middle East working for a European business. The freelance professional is working *from* every continent —and they are working for businesses operating on *every* continent. The virtual office of the Internet provides a new low-overhead office for businesses and freelancers to go "online" together.

As a freelancer, the creation of the world's wealth stands on your able shoulders as you will significantly influence our global economy. The thoughts you will write on paper will move the wheels of wealth creation. The world will continue to progress when you convert your thoughts into stories, plans, designs and perspectives.

Our generation has entered the knowledge economy where creation and utilization of knowledge is the name of the game. Employers are hiring people they have never met and task farms are popping up everyone under the name "crowd-sourcing". This is the rise of the freelance contractor and the trend is skyrocketing all around the world. Entire economies are being uplifted by the outsourcing phenomenon.

Language as well as distance is no longer a barrier only merely a way to categorize available skills and compensation levels. It has crossed geographic borders and has created the global village where ideas and technology are now easily shared.

There is always room for you as a FREELANCER....

## About the Contributors

This book would not have been possible without the contributions of the freelancers in this book.

For more information about the contributors or to contribute your own success story for future publication, please visit:

www.nickpassig.com/resources

## Resources

There are numerous resources on the author's website including:

- freelance marketplaces to find jobs

- contributor biographies and contact information

- additional free resources for building a better freelance and business career

- bonus chapters that were not included in the book

Get access to the book's free resources at:
www.nickpassig.com/resources

Sign up for Nick Passig's Internet Bootcamp:
www.nickpassig.com/vault (it's free)

## About the Author

Nick Passig is an entrepreneur and consultant helping organizations solve business, social and economic challenges using Internet technology.

Mr. Passig's books, software and television programs have been enjoyed by millions of people and have become classics of their kind.

Mr. Passig is owner of Rio World Class and resides in Denver, Colorado.

For more information about the author visit:
www.NickPassig.com

For more information about the publisher visit:
 www.RioWorldClass.com